D1284893

HAVE SALT IN YOURSELVES:

A Book of QuakerPsalms
for Those Called to Holiness and Chastity

From the Journal and Epistles of George Fox

Compiled and Arranged with an Introduction
by T.H.S. Wallace

Foundation Publications
Camp Hill, PA 17011-2947 USA
2010

TABLE OF CONTENTS

How to Make the Most of this Book

HOW TO MAKE THE MOST OF THIS BOOK

When God sows His Seed in us, Jesus tells us it faces many dangers. The very first comes from the devil, "who comes and takes away the word from their hearts, so that they may not believe and be saved." A second danger is that the Seed is not allowed to take firm root and, during a time of testing: the new plant withers. Some fail to mature, because of "the cares and riches and pleasures of life" and thus produce no fruit worthy of repentance. Only those who embrace and hold the word fast in "an honest and good heart...bear fruit with patient endurance." If we cannot hold fast, if we do not endure, we become salt that has lost its savor, salt that is good for nothing but to be thrown out and trod under foot. And Satan would love to be the first to walk all over us.

The problem we face is that at the moment of our being born again, we are all too aware that we have not been living with honest, good hearts, and are rarely ready to be patient and endure. Though our Lord has told us, "in this life you will have troubles," we too often cave at the first sign of those troubles, even though our Lord is present and willing to bring the full power of God to our aid, if we will but fix our attention upon Him and hear His voice. As Paul tells, Christ Jesus is closer than our very breath and whispers to us, "This is the way: walk in it." If we turn not within, if we continue to gaze outward, distracted by the dumb show and thin pleasures of the world, we will soon be weakened, distracted, confused and find ourselves carried away or stunted or wilted by the predations and heat of ordinary life. We will miss the love and power God wants to lavish upon us, so that we may survive and thrive in New Life.

The present little work, *Have Salt in Yourself*, can and will provide both new and veteran Christians with much good counsel, many exhortations and admonitions, so that they may grow in grace. Its subtitle, *A Book of QuakerPsalms for Those Called to Holiness and Chastity*, emphasizes that our work is not only to be born into New Life, but to grow in holiness, in purity of mind, body, and soul – and to live a chaste life. In another age, the faithful would likely say, "doesn't that go without saying?!" But in the Western Cultures of the 21st century, it regrettably *doesn't*. We live in a time when faithfulness is discouraged and mocked, when purity is ridiculed and constantly tempted by insidious and militant evil, and the very institutions of government and "learning" actively deny and denigrate the life of abstinence, self-control, and chastity, claiming them to be the unrealistic values of sick, stunted, and abnormal personalities. Walking the walk – following our Lord Jesus Christ – is every bit as difficult today as it was two thousand years ago in the Empire of Rome. Our own age, like those times, is awash in pagan beliefs and attitudes, strange and deadly religions, and a lust for money and power at any cost - yes, even the cost of one's soul.

However, in the counsel of early Quakers – and especially George Fox, the foremost apostle among them – we can find astute and undiluted spiritual direction that will greatly aid us in living and walking with radical (*radix* = *root*) faithfulness. Known even by their enemies as the most Christian of all Christians in their day, a people of God for whom Christ Jesus was everything, their faithfulness and example still shine across the centuries in the same way the faithfulness and example of the early Christians do.

QuakerPsalms and *Have Salt in Yourselves*
Companion Volumes, but not Identical Twins

Have Salt in Yourselves is a companion volume to *QuakerPsalms: A Book of Devotions,* published in 2002 and reprinted in 2007. *QuakerPsalms* serves as a good introduction to some of the key revelations given by our Lord to George Fox and presents invaluable spiritual and pastoral advice and counsel from his epistles to God's people. The introduction to *QuakerPsalms* specified what was different about it, in contrast to so many books about the spiritual life today:

> *QuakerPsalms* challenge much of what passes for Christianity in our day. The faith that undergirds *QuakerPsalms* is not the weak faith of Puritan England, which preached up the power of sin and denied God's power and love to save men and women from it in this life. The faith witnessed in these psalms is a faith that looks to Jesus Christ for the power to keep His commandments and *finds that power given!* The faith testified to here is one that has the

power to unify Christ's church and overcome all manner of persecution, suffering, and death. These psalms speak of a faith that bears the good fruits of love, meekness, patience, kindness, steadfastness, honesty, and faithfulness – and is identified by those fruits. These psalms testify to a faith that stands for righteousness, opposes deceit, and is utterly resistant to evil, which it fights with spiritual, not physical weapons. *QuakerPsalms* proclaim a faith that seeks the good of all, for God would have all to be saved (*QuakerPsalms: A Book of Devotions,* xi).

Have Salt in Yourselves aims to assist those who have received Christ Jesus into their lives, who have elected to be reborn and grow up as New Men and Women, who would walk in His Light according to His will. It is intended to help them avoid common and dangerous pitfalls in their spiritual lives.

The Four Sections of *Have Salt in Yourselves*

The present book is organized around four key elements of our faith and practice, identifying (1) **the right course of nature to which the Lord calls us,** (2) **how to stand fast in the faith of which Christ Jesus is the author,** (3) **the overwhelming importance of being a member of Christ's body, God's people, the community of faith,** and (4) **the utter importance of seeking the lost by living and proclaiming the good news of Christ Jesus' presence and power.**

The first section, **The Right Course of Nature,** introduces us to some doctrinal essentials of life in Christ. For those who would eschew doctrine, the admonition is don't! What you choose to believe concerning the world, the flesh, and the devil does make a difference, and will lead to different places and outcomes and - at the end of life - to victory or despair and defeat.

The Right Course of Nature beings us back to nature's course as it was before the Fall. This section introduces us to the emblematic nature of salvation history and to the differences in life and action between those who choose to follow Christ Jesus and those who follow Satan. In the latter case, whether the following is overt or covert, the result is the same. By overt, I mean: one willfully chooses the wrong path and defiantly chooses against God. Covert following happens when one simply wanders over to the wrong way by laxness, inattention, and little missteps that lead one closer and closer to the lip of the pit until one has slipped over. This section ends with a consideration of the Cross, and its role in breaking the shackles of sin within us and leading us into righteousness. It is the power of God assisting us in working out our salvation.

Stand Fast in the Faith... presents key considerations that help us stand fast on solid ground, avoiding a world of spiritual quick sand, sand storms, mire, muck, and muddle. This section identifies common errors and missteps we can face in our walk with Christ and it helps us identify what is to be avoided – false steps that scripture and our early Friends were cognizant of. It is full of useful, practical Quaker spirituality.

Foresake Not the Assembling of Yourselves Together... is a key section that emphasizes the simple truth that we cannot live our lives in Christ without others. This simple truth is not so simple for those who live in the highly individualistic cultures of the West, cultures which denigrate or attempt to ignore the necessity and value of community life and the life sustaining spiritual direction that the body of Christ can provide. Those who go it alone become easy prey for the darkness that circles us, seeking to destroy us. Western individualism is the garden plot of insidious pride and fertilizes its noxious undergrowth.

The final section, **Never Give Over Seeking the Lost,** touches on the most neglected aspect for Quaker faith and practice today: the preaching of Christ Jesus' gospel of salvation, sanctification, and peace.

Included in this volume is a short **Appendix of Brief Doctrinals,** small psalms from Fox's doctrinal writings. Readers will find these brief doctrinal psalms extremely cogent and useful in making clear important points of Quaker faith and practice, like the Quaker doctrine of perfection. I have found no better definition of that momentous doctrine than the little statement included in the Appendix (p.100).

How to Read This Book

I have chosen to include here some useful counsel on the best approach to reading the psalms in this book, counsel reprinted from *QuakerPsalms: A Book of Devotions.* "To read these psalms rightly, one must step back from traditional Catholic and Protestant doctrine, for what George Fox is saying here goes back to early Christianity and its foundation: the experience of the risen Christ revealing Himself to His people and directing their work in His world. In fact, when we compare the effects of the early Christian revelation with the early Quaker revelation and witness, we see both possessed a living sense of God's power and love – and the lives of faithful people in both groups bear testimony that indeed their faith was radically different from that of the world around them. Their effect on that world was to turn it upside down by their utter faithfulness. These *QuakerPsalms* witness to the Truth and they have the credentials to prove it."

Have Salt in Yourselves is best read slowly, carefully, contemplatively. Look for gems of observation and advice, unusual and startling phrasings, which speak of a profound experience and understanding of the work of the Spirit. Look for gems and you'll find them in profusion.

Have Salt in Yourselves is meant to be read with the eyes of faith, eyes opened by Jesus Christ to the Truth behind the words. George Fox, himself, observed that words alone are inadequate to communicate the Truth of God. He notes that the Jews of Jesus' time had the scriptures, at least in the form of the Old Testament, but the written words in and of themselves were insufficient to bring them to a recognition of the Christ. Fox compared their experience with that of people in his own time (1630s-1690) and observed "how people read the scriptures without a right sense of them, and without duly applying them to their own states" [*Journal* 31]. Thus, his apostolic mission was:

> To turn people from darkness to the light that they might receive Christ Jesus, for to as many as should receive him in his light, I saw that he would give power to become the sons of God, which I had obtained by receiving Christ. and I was to direct people to the Spirit that gave forth the Scriptures, by which they might be led into all Truth, and so up to Christ and God, as they had been who gave them forth [*Journal* 34].

For Fox and the early Quakers, it was the Spirit that opened the Truth within the words of Scripture, and it should be for us. One cannot rightly and fully understand the Scriptures unless they are "opened" or interpreted by Christ. Seeking our living and present Teacher to reveal the true meaning of Scripture brings us to the true source of authority in things spiritual – not *The Book* alone – but Christ Jesus who interprets it.

What is true of reading the Scriptures is true for reading this little book: See first what Jesus Christ, The Word of God, reveals to you in *Have Salt in Yourselves*. Like Scripture, the psalms here were composed in the Spirit, written to be read and understood on a deeper level than simply the intellectual. They speak of God's and Christ's ongoing revelation of themselves to us and open the momentous possibility of bringing our lives into full communion with, and complete obedience to, our Lord, Creator, and Shepherd.

-T.H.S. Wallace
7ᵗʰ of Fourth Month 2010

The QuakerPsalms that follow are from the 1831 eight volume edition of George Fox's *Works*. Citations to the edition are made at the end of each Psalm by the epistle number (for those drawn from Fox's epistles), volume and page number.

All citations to George Fox's *Journal* are to the John L. Nickalls edition published by the Religious Society of Friends in 1975.

Introduction

In which we consider:
- ➤ *what to do when we have tasted the immediate working power and presence of God and find ourselves beginning to change because of it,*
- ➤ *and how to be established on the foundation of Christ Jesus.*

TO THOSE WHO HAVE TASTED OF THE IMMEDIATE WORKING POWER OF THE LORD AND DO FIND ALTERATION IN YOUR MINDS

Prologue

To all you who have tasted of the immediate
>   working power of the Lord
>   and do find an alteration in your minds
>   and do see whence virtue comes
>   and strength that renews the inward man
>   and refreshes you,
>   which draws you in love to forsake the world
>   and that which has form and beauty in it
>   to the eye of the world:

1

Wait upon God in that which is pure.

Though you see little,
>   and know little,
>   and have little,

and see your emptiness,
>   your nakedness,
>   and barrenness and unfruitfulness,

and see the hardness of your hearts
>   and your own unworthiness:

It is the Light that discovers all this
>   *and the love of God to you.*

It is that which is immediate[1],
    but the dark understanding cannot comprehend it.

2

So wait upon God in that which is pure,
    in your measure.

Stand still in it everyone,
    to see your savior,
        to make you free from that which the Light
            discovers to you to be evil.

The voice of the bridegroom is heard in our land:
    Christ is come among the prisoners,
        to visit them in the prison houses;

They have all hopes of releasement
    and free pardon,
        and to come out freely.

Wait for the manifestation of it,
    and he that comes out of prison shall reign.

Epistle 16, VII:25

---

[1] Immediate = God's Light and love discovers all this   There is no intermediary or intervening member, medium or agent necessary to produce the discovery. In other words, the actual contact with God is direct and personal, not done through a third party, like a priest or a particular ritual or sacrament.

HOW TO BE ESTABLISHED ON THE FOUNDATION OF CHRIST JESUS

The Light & Power & Spirit of God in thee
lets thee see thy hardness, darkness,
thoughts & temptations, & the tempter,
▼
and thy confusion, deadness, & wants
which the bad spirit persuades thee to look out[2] at.
▼
Then thou murmurs, complains, & are discontent, & not quiet.
▼
Then the enemy and death cover thee
and thy mind comes to be *unestablished.*
Therefore keep to the good spirit in thee
which does manifest sin and the devil.
Thy mind being staid by that,
it will inform[3] thee.
▼
Keep thy mind in the seed (in that is thy life)
& look at the good,
not at the bad, but over it,
▼
for it is not a sin to be tempted
and that which the accuser lays to thee
and thy mind being against it
and not yielding to it,
it will never be laid to thy charge.
Doubt not, faint not, question not,
for Eve was deceived by the serpent, the questioner.

---

[2] Look out = means being influenced by the outward, by the world and its values and events, instead of seeking to hear and know Christ Jesus alive and working within us, directing us to what is true and right.

[3] Inform = this word means far more than simply to give information or knowledge; it means that the New Man or Woman will be formed in us as we keep to our spiritual Guide.

▼

Therefore keep over him in God's power
& in that thou reigns.
Take not thy belief from the serpent nor take meat from him.

▼

Keep thy fast from that which is in the fall,
for that brings [people away] from the Lord
to feed upon the accuser and the tempter's food
that feeds unbelief.

▼

Keep thy fast to the Lord
& feed upon that which comes down from above
& that strengthens faith which has victory.

The Right Course of Nature

In which we consider:
➤ *The original of all language, Christ Jesus, the Word of God and what He does,*
➤ *What the right course of our nature is,*
➤ *What the true and standing religion is and what it does,*
➤ *How Salvation History figures forth our individual spiritual history,*
➤ *What the differences are between the children of God and the children of Satan,*
➤ *and the work of Christ's cross in our salvation.*

THE ORIGINAL OF ALL LANGUAGE

The Word of God[4] is the original,
    which fulfills the scriptures.

The Word is it which makes divine,[5]
    is called a hammer,
        but it is a living hammer;
    a sword and fire,
        but it is a living sword
          and a living fire –
    a hammer, sword, and fire
        to hammer, and cut down, and burn up
          that which separated and kept man from God.

By this Word man is reconciled again to God,
    which [Word] is called the Word of Reconciliation.
By this Word are men and women sanctified and made clean.

This is the Word that makes both men and women divine,
    brings them into the divine nature,
        hammers and cuts down that which
          corrupted their nature.

---

[4] *The Word of God* refers to Christ Jesus, not to His scriptures. See the last line of this QuakerPsalm or the 1st chapter of the Gospel of John. Those Protestants who term the scriptures The Word of God may be confused by the Quaker claim that The Word of God is Christ Jesus. However, the Quakers – not the Protestants – are correct, for the scriptures themselves identify Christ Jesus as The Word, both in the first chapter of John's Gospel and in The Revelation of John 19:13

[5] *divine* = Could be used in any or all of several senses: Divine as in "makes godly;" Divine as in "makes prophetic;" or "makes discovery" [OED]. It is unlikely to be a misprint that should simply read "a divine." While Friends recognized that Jesus Christ selected men and women and made them ministers of His gospel, such ministers were not in the habit of calling themselves "divines" nor did their hearers refer to them as "divines." "Divine" seems to fit the context better – in the sense that our Lord makes His people "godly." See stanza 3 as further confirmation that this is how the word is being used.

By this Word are they brought into a divine wisdom,
    understanding, knowledge, spirit, and power.

This is the Word that lives and abides and endures forever,
    by which the saints are born again of the immortal Seed and Word of
        God – [the saints] who feed upon the milk of the Word
            up into a divine life, wisdom, understanding,
                and divine nature.

By this Word they do see all flesh to be as grass,
    and as the flower of the field that fades.
The Word of God that lives and abides and endures forever
    is Christ, whose name is called the Word of God.

THE RIGHT COURSE OF NATURE

You that are enlightened with the Light that comes from Jesus,
    to it take heed: it leads into the right course of nature.

You who act contrary to it go out of the right course of nature
    into drunkenness, rashness, lying,
    blaspheming, deceit, and uncleanness.

All this leads out of the right course of nature
    and destroys it. All this is to be condemned
    with that which leads to the glory of the first body,[6]

and leads nature into its right course and right being,
    which man was in before he fell.

-Epistle 28, VII:35

---

[6]first body = the pure body of Adam before he fell.

THERE IS A SUMMER RELIGION[7]

There is a summer religion
which appears when the sun shines.
All the venomous creatures creep
out of their holes, corners, and dens,
and the flies, wasps and snakes;

but when the winter is come
and the storms and tempests come,
then the summer religion is gone,
then the venomous, viperous creatures'
religion and works are gone.

But the religion in the power of God stands,
which was before the devil was
and all his works and children.
That is the standing religion
that is in the power of God which
was before the power of darkness.

-Epistle 205, VII:200-201

---

[7] There are two religions we face, a false summer religion and a true religion standing in God's power. The former leads to false faith, the latter to God's love, direction, and way. The perception of the existence of the two religions is a key point of Quaker understanding and spiritual experience. It can also be found throughout the scriptures in the struggle between those of true faith and those espousing false religion, a struggle that is shot through the scriptures from Genesis to Revelation. Christ Jesus Himself warns us that there will be weeds among the wheat and that He will separate the two at harvest – that we are not to try to banish the weeds during the growing season for fear of harming the wheat.

SALVATION HISTORY

"I saw also how people read the Scriptures
without a right sense of them, and without
duly applying them to their own states."
-The Journal of George Fox, Nickalls edition, p.30

When they read that death reigned from Adam to Moses,
and the Law and the prophets were until John,
and that the least in the kingdom is greater than John:

    they read these things without them[8]
    and applied them to others without them,
    and these things were true of others,
    but they did not turn in to find the truth
    of these things with themselves.

As these things came to be opened[9] to me, I saw

    Death reigned over them from Adam to Moses:
        that from the entrance into transgression
        till they came to the ministration of condemnation,
        which restrains people from sin that brings death.

    Then the ministration of Moses is passed through,
        the ministry of the prophets comes to be read
        and understood, which reaches through
        the figures, types, and shadows[10] unto John,

---

[8] Without them = Instead of looking for the truth of salvation history in their own lives, as emblematic of their spiritual growth and development, they applied it outwardly to history in general, to other peoples and individuals, other times and places.

[9] opened = revealed by God

[10] Types, figures, and shadows = It is very important that readers understand this reference much more fully. See Appendix 1 for a more complete discussion. This phrase refers to "typology, the practice in both the New Testament and the early church whereby a person or a series of events occurring in the Old Testament is interpreted as

the greatest prophet born of woman,
whose ministration prepares the way of the Lord
by bringing down the exalted mountains
and making straight paths.
And as this ministration is passed through,
entrance comes to be known into the everlasting kingdom.

I saw none could read Moses aright without Moses' spirit,
by which Moses saw
how man was in the image of God in paradise,
how he fell and how death came over him, and
how all men have been under this death.

I saw how Moses received the pure Law
that went over all transgressors,
how the clean beasts which were figures and types
were offered up when the people were come
into the righteous Law that went over the first transgression.

And both Moses and the prophets saw
through the types and figures,
and beyond them, and saw Christ
the great prophet that was to come
to fulfill them.

I saw none would read John's words[11] aright
and with a true understanding of them,
but the same divine Spirit by which John spoke them,
and by His burning, shining light,
which was sent from God.
By that spirit their crooked natures might be made straight,
their rough natures smooth, and the exacter
and violent doer in them might be thrown out,

---

a type or foreshadowing of some person (almost invariably Christ) or feature of the
Christian interpretation" [*The Oxford Companion to the Bible,* pp.783-784].
[11]John's words = refers to John the Baptist's words, not the writer of the Gospel of
John, the Letters, and the Revelation..

and they that had been hypocrites might come
to bring forth fruits of repentance
and their mountain of sin and earthliness
might be laid low in them,
and their valley exalted in them,
that there might be a way prepared for the Lord in them –
and then the least in the kingdom is greater than John –

But ALL must FIRST know the voice crying in the wilderness
of their hearts (which through transgression
were become as a wilderness).[12]

As man comes through by the Spirit and power of God to Christ –
who fulfills the types, figures shadows, promises and prophecies
that were of Him – and is led by the Holy Ghost into the truth
and substance of Scriptures,
sitting down in Him who is the author and end of them,
then are they read and understood with profit and delight.

Now the Lord God opened to me by his invisible power
how that every man was enlightened by the divine Light of Christ.
I saw it shine through all,
    and that they that believed in it came out of condemnation
        and came to the Light of life
           and became children of it,

but they that hated it and did not believe in it
    were condemned by it,
        though they made a profession of Christ,

for I saw in that Light and Spirit
    which was before Scripture was given forth,
        and which led the holy men of God to give them forth,

---

[12] "Prepare the way for the Lord, make straight paths for him," John the Baptist's words
calling the people to prepare for the coming of Christ Jesus.

that ALL must come to that Spirit,
   if they would know God or Christ,
      or the Scriptures aright,
      which they that gave them forth
      were led and taught by.

ON THE NATURE OF THE DEVIL'S CHILDREN AND GOD'S

1

The children of the devil,
    how expert are they in evil,
        in all deceit in his kingdom –

        and yet they may speak
        of the things of God:

but no vulturous eye or venomous beast
    ever trod in the steps of the just,
        though they may talk of the way.

Who have their conversation in this world
    and only mind the things of this world,
        in vain do they profess godliness.

But the children of God,
    conceived and begotten by Him,
        are not of this world,

neither do they mind only
    the things of this world,
        but the things which are eternal.

The children of the world do
    mostly mind the external things
        and their love is in them.

The other live by faith.
    The one is sanctified by the Word,
        the other painted with the words.

The favor of the world
    and the friendship thereof
        is enmity to God.

Man may soon be stained with it.
    Oh! Love the stranger.
        Be as strangers in and to the world!

For they that followed Christ in His cross,
    they were strangers to the world,
        wonders to the world,
            and condemned by the world.

2

The world knew Him not,
neither does it them that follow Him now,
so marvel not if the world hate you,
for the world lies in hatred and wickedness.

Who love this world are enemies of Christ;
and who love the Lord Jesus Christ,
and have Him for their Lord over them,
they are redeemed out of the world.

The world would have a Christ,
but not to rule over them.
The nature of the world is above
Christ in man, until Christ
has subdued that nature in man.

While the nature of the world rules in man,
Oh! The deaf ears and blind eyes,
and the understandings
that are all shut up among them,
with which they judge!

3

But who love the Lord Jesus Christ
do not mind the world's judgment,
nor are troubled at it,
but consider all our brethren
who have gone before us.

When you think you are past all crosses,[13]
when the trial comes,
you will find a cross to that will
which meddles with the things of God
presumptuously: you may live in joy,
but your spirit is in bondage.

Rejoice not in the flesh, but in the Spirit
which crucifies all fleshly boasting:
if the fleshly will be fed,
then carelessness comes up
and they fall into flatness (from the Spirit)
and are mindless of the Lord God.
Such are soon up and down.

The serpent tempted Eve to eat
of the forbidden fruit,
and she took and gave to her husband,
and so they fell under the serpent's power

---

[13] A principle of Quaker faith is that no one graduates from the school of Christ Jesus, our teacher in this life. The presumptuous error here is in thinking one can get past all crosses in this life. Since the inward cross is a key guide in our walk with Christ Jesus, to think we can escape it or no longer need it is the height of prideful presumption. Thus, when we meet a new trial or trouble in life, that trial or trouble will be a cross to our presumption of getting beyond the need for God's guidance. Even if we bravely still claim spiritual joy, we have in reality fallen back into spiritual bondage. The stanza following this one accurately charts how we drift back into mindlessness of God.

and the creatures, out of the power of God[14]
which would have kept them in dominion.

So, Adam and Eve and the serpent
all went out of Truth.
Eve eating of the tree of knowledge,
she had knowledge and wisdom after the Fall,
but not the dominion in the power of God.
But the seed Christ, which was in the beginning,
bruises the serpent's head,
and He is the wisdom of God.

-Epistle 2, VII:16-17

---

[14]Adam and Eve fell not only under the serpent's power, but also under the creatures, instead of having dominion over them in God's power. This is not a surprising result, since we all have been at one time or other in our lives under the domination of things – possessions, drugs, food, etc.

CONCERNING THE CROSS OF CHRIST

The cross is to[15] the carnal part, the ground
of images, the ground of the seducers,
the ground of the false prophet and antichrist:[16]
to that ground, to the root and life of it.

This[17], which is pure and eternal, being minded,
it makes a separation from all other lovers,
and brings to God. The ground of evil thoughts
comes to be opened – the cross is to that ground.

The cross overturns the world in the heart,
which cross must be taken up by all
who follow Jesus Christ out of the world
which has an end, into the world without end.

All the evil things of the world must be
denied, for 'who loves the world, the love
of the Father is not in him' – where the world
is standing, the cross is not lived in.

But dwelling in the cross to the world, here
the love of God is shed abroad in the heart.
The way is opened into the inheritance
which fades not away, where nothing

---

[15] To = as in to expose, subdue, and destroy.
[16] Here are listed key purposes of the cross within: it exposes the feeble foundation of images and idols that would usurp God's place, the false foundation of seducers and their arguments, the poisonous nature of the ground from which false prophets and antichrists spring.
[17] This = This cross.

shall enter which is defiled, for God is
not seen but in the eternal light whence
all pure wisdom comes. This treasure
is not seen, but with the spiritual eye,

nor received but with the pure in heart,
and by those who dwell and abide in the
eternal light. The carnal heart may get
the words from them who had received wisdom,

who dwelt in the fear of the Lord, but they
who live without the fear may get their words
and yet know not wisdom's gate, whence those words
proceeded. They have the old bottle.[18]

Watch all, therefore, and see what you possess,
for all who gave forth the holy scripture,
who dwelt in the fear of God, they possessed
the life which those words proceeded from

and the secrets of the Lord were with them.
Therefore, all in your measure which is of God,
wait, that it may guide your minds up to God,
and follow it and not your evil desires,

nor the lust of the world, for the fear[19] of the Lord
will keep your hearts clear and the true wisdom
will be with you in the pure heart. Everyone
that has this light, which Christ has enlightened

---

[18]the old bottle = perhaps a reference to what the Geneva Bible, which Fox used,
termed vessels, and which modern translations term wineskins. It could also be a
reference to the "earthen vessels" into which our Lord pours His Spirit, the precious
treasure. "Old bottle" might refer to the "old man" or "old woman," our old nature,
whereas the new bottle would be the new nature, the vessel transformed by the
presence and will of Christ Jesus.
[19] Fear = awe

them withal, the deeds that are evil you know
to be so by the light – and this light will be their
condemnation. You know it. And all who witness
this light and love it, their eye is in their head,

which is Christ, if they be ten thousands.[20]

-Epistle 51, 7:66-67

---

[20] Those who witness God's light and love, their eye is located in their head, Christ
Jesus, the head of the Church, even if they number in the tens of thousands. This
sentence describes the spiritual unity that Christ Jesus brings us into.

Stand Fast in the Faith of Which Christ Jesus is the Author

To stand fast in the faith which Christ authors, we examine:
➢ *What we must do when we have tasted the direct working power of God,*
➢ *How we must live in His unchangeable life and power,*
➢ *How we are called to holiness and chastity,*
➢ *How we must keep our minds in the Almighty's strength,*
➢ *Have salt in ourselves and be low in heart,*
➢ *Beware of discouraging any in the work of God,*
➢ *Encourage all women,*
➢ *Know the praying in the spirit,*
➢ *And abide in our calling.*

YOU WHO HAVE TASTED OF THE IMMEDIATE POWER OF THE LORD

Wait upon God in that which is pure,
    you who have tasted of the immediate
    working power of the Lord.
Wait upon God in that which is pure,
    you who do find an alteration in your minds,
    and do see from whence virtue comes
    and strength that renews the inward man
    and refreshes you, which draws you
    to forsake the world and that which has
    form and beauty in it to the eye of the world.

Wait upon God, you who have tasted of the Lord's
    immediate, working power
    and have turned your minds within,
    who see your houses foul and corruptions strong,
    and the Way narrow and straight that leads
    to life eternal. Wait upon God.

Though you see little, and know little and have little,
and see your emptiness, your nakedness, barrenness,
and unfruitfulness, and see the hardness of your hearts,
and your own unworthiness, it is the light that discovers
this and the love of God to you. It is that which is
immediate, but the dark understanding cannot comprehend it.

So wait upon God in that which is pure, in your measures,
    and stand still in it every one, to see your savior,
    to make you free from that which the light
    does discover to you to be evil,
    for the voice of the bridegroom is heard in our land
    and Christ is come among the prisoners,
    to visit them in the prison houses.

They have all hopes of releasement and free pardon,
and to come out freely, for the debt is paid.

Wait for the manifestation of it
and he that comes out of prison shall reign.

-Epistle 16, VII:24

LIVE IN THE UNCHANGEABLE
LIFE AND POWER

Live in the unchangeable power, life,
    and seed of God.

Be out of the world's low, earthly spirit
    given to changing and tossing, tempests
        and waves by which the dirt is cast up.

Oh, live in the life and power of God and His seed,
    which never change, by which everyone
        may stand in God's power and in His life,
            and wisdom through which you may all live.

Stand steadfast in the unchangeable life and seed of God,
    which was before changings and altering were
        and which remains when they all are gone.

God Almighty in that preserve you,
    in which you may have blessings among you,
        and God's wisdom to order you to His glory,

that so in His fear you may be preserved to God's glory,
    in His wisdom and life in that which does not change,
        in which you may feel the unchangeable fellowship.

And Friends: Be wise and low.
    Take heed of abusing God's power,
        but live in it, in the still life, patient,

to the answering the good in all,
    to the refreshing one of another,
        and not to the stumbling.

But mind that which keeps in unity,
    in the life,
        though never so little.[21]

-VII:86

---

[21] Though never so little = a point George Fox often makes. Sometimes God's presence and power seem very weak, but they are not. They are overwhelmingly powerful, so we should mind "that which keeps in unity" and "in the life."

YOU ARE CALLED TO HOLINESS AND CHASTITY

You who have tasted of the love, mercy,
and kindness of God, and His power,
you are called to holiness and chastity.

Therefore keep out of inordinate affections[22]
and inordinate fleshly love, a feigned flattery
and desires which are below the Truth –
[desires] which will bring you to infirmness.

Keep out of fond affections[23] and fond love,
that draw out the fleshly part, the fleshly eye,
and bring into pride, and looseness,
and false liberty – and to abuse God's power.

Keep out of all uncleanness and fleshy desires,
whatever may be pretended, for the
'lust[24] of the eye, the lust of the flesh, and the pride
of life are not of the Father, but of the world.'

Therefore keep down that which is not of the Father,
but of the world. Take heed of dishonoring your bodies
and defiling your minds, but keep your bodies clean
from all fornication, adultery, and uncleanness –

---

[22] inordinate affections = not ordered; devoid of order or regularity; deviating from right and rule; irregular, disorderly; not regulated; not kept within orderly limits, intemperate, excessive (OED)

[23] fond affection, fond love = in the 17th century "fond" was a derogatory description. It meant foolish, credulous, infatuated, silly, and under some circumstances, mad, dazed, idiotic; valued only by fools, trifling, trivial.

[24] Lust = intense desires that are morally reprobate.

for that which pretends[25] otherwise, and does so,
defiles it and is out of the Truth, is contrary
to the law of God, and contrary to Christ's doctrine.
Therefore defile not yourselves,

but live pure, chaste, and holy, as becomes the saints,
for no adulterer nor fornicator has any part in God's kingdom.
Such go from that of God in themselves, quench
God's spirit, and abuse His power, and go into fleshly love,

feigned desires, and flattering pretenses, covering them
with a false liberty – and so are in the bondage to the beggarly,
fleshly lusts. Whom they overcome, they bring into the same bondage,
and through their feigned flattery and dissembling carriage,

rob and beguile and spoil to fulfill their insatiable
ungodly desires, wills, and lust.
Therefore live in the Truth,
for all such things are out of the Truth

and such as do the same, whatsoever they be.
Therefore all who go into uncleanness
under what fair pretense so ever,
are to be judged.

-Epistle 168, VII:156

---

[25] Pretends = professes or designs.

KEEP YOUR MINDS IN THE
ALMIGHTY'S STRENGTH

All dwell in God's everlasting seed, Christ
Jesus, in whom you have health and strength, life
and dominion, and power over all weaknesses.
Keep your minds in the Almighty's strength,
and not in weakness, nor in the infirmities,
but in the Lord's power, which was before
weakness and infirmities were.

In that power you will find life
and refreshment from the God of strength.
So in God's power that is over all,
keep your minds in God's life and peace,
and in the assurance of Him and His love.
In that dwell, and live in God's dominion,
in His love, and life, and strength.

Be of good faith, and of a valiant mind
for God's Truth upon the earth, in the power,
life, Truth, and seed, in which you have dominion,
peace, wisdom, and God's blessing upon you,
and in you; and in that dwell, and know that
blessed seed your crown and life.

-Epistle 159, VII:151

HAVE SALT IN YOURSELVES AND
BE LOW IN HEART

Have salt in yourselves and be low in heart.
The light is low[26] in you. It will teach you
to be low, teach you to learn that lesson
of Jesus Christ, to the plucking down
all the high thoughts and imaginations.

Take heed of strife in your minds.
If there be[27], then glory not, for it is
the vain mind and it is not good.
Let no strife be among you.
Let none seek for the highest place,

for there is the separated[28] Pharisee,
but be lowly-minded, condescending[29]
one to another in a low degree.
Bear one with another in patience
and be not high minded, but fear.[30]

---

[26] The light is low = it is humble. See Philippians 2:5-11.

[27] If there be = if there be strife

[28] Separated Pharisee = the separated Pharisee is symbolic of religious persons who deemed themselves righteous in their own conduct and life and who seek and expect praise, recognition, and honors they feel are due them. The Pharisees separated themselves from the common run of humanity, thanking God they were not like other men and women, "sinners." Fox is exhorting Christians to avoid those with such attitudes and live in the humility of Christ Jesus.

[29] Condescending = in 17th century England, this term meant "gracious, considerate, or submissive deference shown to another" (OED).

[30] fear = If one stands in awe of the Lord's astonishing power, one will naturally feel one's own insignificance, one's own nothingness. Fear here means to stand in awe, the antidote to high-mindedness.

All who are servants, labor in love,
as unto God, for 'the earth is the Lord's
and the fullness thereof.' Labor in singleness
as unto the Lord. And all who have families,
rule in the power and love of God, that

that love may be head among you.

-Epistle 79, VII:90

BEWARE OF DISCOURAGING ANY IN
THE WORK OF GOD

Mind that which is pure in you to guide you to God,
    out of Babylon,[31] out of confusion.

    There all the world is. There is the beast's seat.
    There are the false prophets and deceivers,
    as well within as without.
    One voice of deceit knows not another,
    nor any of them the voice of the living God.

But, dear Friends, mind the Light of God in your consciences,
    which will show you all deceit. Dwelling in it
    guides out of the many things into one Spirit,
    which can not lie nor deceive.
    They that are guided by it are one,
    who have been made to drink into one Spirit,
    and the spirits of the prophets are subject to the prophets.
    God is not the author of confusion, but of peace.

All jarrings, all schisms, all rents are out of the Spirit,
    for God has tempered the body together,
    that there should be no schism,
    but all worship Him with one consent.
    As the power and life of Truth are made manifest,
    watch in the discerning one over another.

Beware of discouraging any in the work of God:
The laborers are few that are faithful for God.
Take heed of hurting the gift,
which God has given to profit withal,
whereby you have received life through death,[32]
and a measure of peace by the destruction of evil.

---

[31] Babylon = slavery.

[32] Received life through death = Not only Christ's death on the cross, but also the death of our Old Self.

Pray, that peace may be multiplied
    and the ministration of life,
    to the raising of the dead,
    that "the seed of the woman may bruise the serpent's head,
    discover all deceit, rend all veils and coverings,[33]
    that the pure may come to life
    which deceit has trampled upon.

All take need to your spirits.

---

[33] Veils and coverings = the seed of the woman that bruises the serpent's head is Christ, who also rends all veils and coverings that cover our hearts and obscure the truth. "When anyone turns to the Lord, the veil is taken away…and we, who with unveiled faces all reflect the Lord's glory, are being transformed into his likeness with ever increasing glory, which comes from the Lord, who is the Spirit" (2 Cor. 3:7-18).

ENCOURAGE ALL THE WOMEN

Encourage all the women of families
that are convinced and mind virtue, love, Truth,
and walk in it, that they come up into God's
service, that they may be serviceable
in their generation and in the creation,
and come into the practice of pure religion,
which you have received from God from above,
that everyone may know their duty in it,
and their service in God's power and wisdom:
for know the practical part is called for.

People must not be always talking and hearing,
but they must come into obedience to the power
of the God of heaven and earth. None should
stand out of the vineyard idle, out of service,
out of their duty, for such will talk and tattle,
and judge with evil thoughts of what they
in the vineyard say and do. God's power
must call all into their duty, into their service,
into their places, into virtue and righteousness,
and into God's wisdom, for God's power must
go over and is over all such, by which power
all must be acted and true obedience known.

-Epistle 296, VIII:65

KNOW THE PRAYING IN THE SPIRIT

Know the praying in the Spirit
and with the understanding.

Then you will come to know the sighs
and groans that cannot be uttered.

> Such as have not the Spirit that gave
> forth the scriptures to guide them
> are as the Pharisees were,
> in the long prayers,
> in the wrath and doubting
> and do not lift up holy hands.
> This makes the difference
> between the praying in the Spirit,
> and the Pharisees' long prayers,
> the Pharisees that devoured widow's houses.

None owns the Light as it is Jesus,
but he that owns the Light
that Christ lights him withal.

None owns the Truth,
but owns the Light that
comes from Christ the Truth.

And none comes to the Father,
but such who own the Light that
comes from Christ, which leads to Him.
And none owns the Son, except
he owns the Light that comes from Him.[34]

---

[34] Notice the utter centrality of Jesus Christ to Quaker spiritual life.

For all dwelling in the Light that comes from Jesus,
it leads out of wars, strife, and the earth,
out of earthly-mindedness to heavenly mindedness,
and brings your minds to God and to be in heaven.

-Epistle 139, VII:133-134

TO ALL – ABIDE IN YOUR CALLINGS (I)

To all dear Friends,
    who are called, who are enlightened,
    whose minds are turned from the world's worships and teachers,
    having your eye to the Light and Guide within
    which is leading you out of this dark world
    and your old vain conversations,
    towards God and the world without end,
mercy and peace from God the Father be multiplied among you!

Every one of you abide in your calling,
waiting upon God where He has called you.

Take heed of reasoning with flesh and blood,
for there disobedience, pride, and presumption
will arise – a fig tree which bears leaves
and no fruit – wells without water!

Oh! Therefore, mind the pure, which will lead you out
of this corruptible, heathenish, dark world, and its
vain ways, and from destruction and death, to life.

So the Lord God of power bless you, guide you,
    preserve you on in your way towards the holy city,
    being called out of the unholy city –
    for He that has called you is holy.
Now many are called but few are chosen!

Oh! Therefore, abide in that which has called you,
that which is holy and pure, up to Him
who is holy and pure.

Let your time past of your evil ways be sufficient,[35]
wherein you have lived in wickedness
and in the ways of this untoward generation,
lest your minds turn back into Egypt and the world
and so cause the Lord's worthy name to be blasphemed
by turning aside and growing into hardness of heart,

turning from a pure conscience and making
shipwreck of it and of faith. You may see
how far many may go and did go and were led out
of many things, *yet did turn again into the world.*

So mind your present Guide,
    your present condition,
    your call, what you were called from,
    and what you are called to,
    for those the Lord has called and chosen
    are the Lord's freemen and freewomen.

So abide everyone in your calling with God,
    where God has called you,
    and there walk in newness of life,
    not in the oldness of the letter,
    for he that turns from Him that calls,
    walks not in God's life.

Therefore, walk in the Truth and in the love of it up to God.
    Everyone in particular mind your Guide,
    that you may grow up in wisdom
    and improve your own talents
    and the gift which God has given you.

---

[35] In other words, that's enough! Put your evil ways behind you. "Sufficient" as used here means "enough" (OED).

Take heed of words without life,
    for they may draw you out of the power
    to live above Truth and out of your conditions,
    which nature will not have peace except it have words.

Submit in every particular to that which is of God in you
    to guide you to God. Be all servants of the Truth,
    diligent in your callings and serve one another in love
    in which you can wash one another's feet.
    Serve one another in love and do not lavish out yourselves
    without the fear of God. Such are clouds flown up
    into the air without water, which have the words
    but not the power, which have a light and yet are
    as wandering stars which lead up to presumption.
    You that are there: Your garments are defiled
    for you go from the Spirit which should sanctify you,
    for you can only be sanctified through obedience to that Spirit.

Therefore [in] every particular: walk in the Spirit and obey it.
Then you will all have unity one with another in the Spirit.
You will see knowledge, tongues and prophecies shall cease,
but he is blessed that comes to the end – to Him who opens all Truth.[36]

-Epistle 79, 7:88-89

---

[36] The end being Christ Jesus who reveals all Truth.

ABIDE IN YOUR CALLINGS (II)

Obey that which is pure within you
and know one another in that which
brings you to wait upon the Lord,
that you may all witness a living soul[37]
and yourselves to be come out of death.

These things you must all find within.
    There is your peace and there refreshing
    comes into your souls from the Lord.
    Standing still in the Light within,
    and therein waiting,
    you will see your savior, Christ Jesus
    raising you up out of death,
    by which work He is glorified
    (for the works of the Lord, which are
    wondrous to the world, praise Him).

Now everyone in particular, mind the pure in you,
for the chaste virgins follow Jesus Christ,
the Lamb of God, who takes away the sins of the world.

Who are not chaste, will not follow Him,
    for that in every particular of you which is not chaste
    will not submit to the pure which would guide you to God,
    but rather submit to their own thoughts
    and follow them and run after them
    and their own wills and seek to accomplish them –
    and so run out into that generation
    whose thoughts were not as God's thoughts
    nor ways as God's ways.

---

[37] Testify that you have a living soul, not a dead one.

Therefore, all of you watch and abide in your callings.
The Light is that which will let you see your transgression
and your running aside, and the bypaths and crooked ways
and the generation of serpents and vipers –
and this is the Light of Christ which shows these things.

Now before these things be known and judged aright,
judgment must be brought forth into victory
and set up in the earth where this[38] state is witnessed.

-Epistle 79, VII:89

---

[38] This final stanza is poorly rendered, but essentially means that before we can know
and judge the things and actions in our lives rightly, God's judgment within us must
progress forward to victory and be established in our earthy being. "This state" may
either refer to the state of transgression we came out of or to the state of living in the
Light of Christ. Both interpretations seem to fit equally well.

STAND FAST IN THE FAITH WHICH CHRIST IS THE AUTHOR OF

Stand by His heavenly ensign in your heavenly armor,
your feet shod with the preparation of the heavenly gospel
of peace,[39] your heads preserved with the helmet of salvation,
and your hearts fenced with the breastplate of righteousness.

Stand feeling and seeing God's banner of love over your heads,
manifesting that you are the good ground that brings forth
fruits in some sixty, some a hundred fold in this life,
to the praise and glory of God, always beholding

the sun of righteousness that never sets, ruling
the supernatural day, of which you are children.
The persecutor's sun, which rises and sets again:
the heat of it cannot scorch your blade, which

it may do that seed that grows on the stony ground.
Therefore, be valiant for God's Truth upon the earth.
Fear Him[40] that can break their fetters, their jails,
their bonds in sunder, and can make your fleece

grow again, after the wolves have torn the wool
from your backs. Hold fast the hope, sure and steadfast,
that anchors the soul, so you may float above the world's sea,
for your anchor holds sure and steadfast in the bottom.

Let the winds, storms and raging waves rise never
so high, your star is fixed by which you may steer
to the eternal land of rest and kingdom of God,
steer to the eternal kingdom of God.

-Epistle 314, 8:73-74

---

[39] The preparation of the heavenly gospel of peace = Ephesians 6:15 – words of *The Geneva Bible* (1560 edition), which Fox used. The "preparation" is so "ye may be ready to suffer all things for the Gospel."
[40] Or stand in awe of Him.

Forsake Not the Assembling of Yourselves Together

In which we continue to examine:
What we must do to stand fast in Christ Jesus:
➤ *How we must not forsake assembling with Christ's people,*
➤ *How we must be a peculiar people of tenderness, and*
➤ *Stand in that which takes away the occasion for wars,*
➤ *While engaging in spiritual warfare,*
➤ *Avoiding running on in a form,*
➤ *Avoiding falling out of unity and denying all forms,*
➤ *How we are to be joined one to another in Christ's body,*
➤ *And keep in His wisdom and life.*

FORSAKE NOT THE ASSEMBLING OF YOURSELVES TOGETHER

Forsake not the assembling of yourselves together
 as the manner of some was in the beginning
 of the apostasy, who entered the reasoning part,
 and went so from the exhorting daily,
 and the building, and the fellowship,
 and the communion of the saints in the Spirit,
 and from the flocks, and the garden of God
 which He waters with His water of life,
 and feeds with His bread of life;
 and sets open His broad rivers of living water to drink.

Such as forsake the assemblies of the righteous
 (some for fear of the earth and sufferings),
 become quarrelling spirits and so go out
 of the path of the flock's footsteps,
 and sit not down with the flock at noon-day
 in the heavenly places of Christ Jesus –

 for there the flocks meet,
 and there they have all a fountain,
 through which they are all of one soul
 and mind and judgment and heart and spirit,
 and come to be gathered out of all the separations
 and sects and fellowships and gatherings
 and meetings of Adam and Eve in the Fall
 and sit down in Christ Jesus that never fell,
 where the fullness is and the life.

-Epistle 232, VII:249-250

THAT YOU MAY BE A PECULIAR PEOPLE IN TENDERNESS

Dwell in the love and life and power of the Lord God,
in the power, life, and seed which have no end
and in which you may all have unity.

Be faithful and dliligent in the things that are good.
Keep your meetings and meet together
in the power of the Lord which cannot be broken,
in which is an everlasting unity.
Live in peace and unity one with another
and all keep in the power of the Lord God.

Take heed of getting into a form without the power,
for that will bring deadness and coldness and weariness,
and fainting, and what will it not bring in that nature!

Therefore keep in the power of the Lord,
which will keep all the contrary down and out
and preserve you in peace and life and unity,
fresh and fruitful and diligent in the wisdom
of the Lord God, with which and in which
you may be kept and preserved to His glory.

Be a good savor to Him and in the hearts of all people,
that to the Lord you may be a blessing in your generation
and a peculiar people in tenderness, and full of that faith

which overcomes the world and all things in it,
through which you may come up into the unity
of the Spirit which is the bond of peace. Yes,
live in the power of the Lord God and keep down
the wise part, which will judge Truth to be simple
and come to despise it and cry up their own words
of wisdom in its place.

-Epistle 180, 7:170

STAND IN THAT WHICH TAKES AWAY
THE OCCASION OF WARS

All Friends everywhere, who are dead to all
carnal weapons and have beaten them to pieces,
stand in that which takes away the occasion of wars,[41]
in the power which saves men's lives and destroys
none, nor would have others [destroy].

As for the rulers that are to keep peace,
for peace's sake and the advantage of Truth,
give them their tribute[42]. But to bear and carry
weapons to fight with, the men of peace
(who live in that which takes away the occasion of wars),

they cannot act in such things under the several powers
but have paid their tribute - which they may do still
for peace sake, and not hold back the earth,[43]
but go over it – and in so doing,
Friends may better claim their liberty.

-Epistle 195, VII:168-169

---

[41] That which takes away the occasion of wars = the Seed, the Truth, Christ Jesus.

[42] Tribute = gift; a payment, declaration, or other acknowledgement of gratitude, respect, or admiration; evidence attesting to some praiseworthy quality or characteristic.

[43] Earth = this term may refer to several things: "the world on which we dwell"; "the present abode of man, in contrast to heaven or hell"; dust or clay; dull, dead matter. It is used here in a spiritual sense: Friends will not be refusing to participate in the world, but will be "going over it," rising beyond it.

CONCERNING SPIRITUAL WARFARE

*The word of the Lord God to all my brethren, babes, and soldiers
who are in the spiritual warfare of our Lord Jesus Christ:*

Arm yourselves like men of war,
that you may know what to stand against.

> Spare not, pity not that which is for the sword
> of the spirit, plague, and famine.
> Set up Truth, and confound the deceit, deceit
> that stains the earth and cumbers the ground.
> > The dead stinks upon the earth
> > and with it the earth is stained.
> > Therefore, bury it.

> Wait in the light which comes from Jesus,
> > to be clothed with His zeal,
> > to stand against all them who act contrary
> > to the light which comes from Jesus
> > and yet profess the words declared from the light –
> > who are sayers but not doers.

> All such are to be trodden without the city under foot
> > and woe proceeds from the Lord against all such.
> > The stone is falling upon such, and fallen,
> > to grind them to powder.

Arm yourselves like men of war.
> The mighty power of God goes along with you,
> to enable you to stand over all the world
> and spiritually to chain, fetter, bind, and imprison –
> and lead out of prison;
> to famish, feed, and to make fat
> and bring into green pastures.

So the name and power of the Lord Jesus Christ be with you!
    Go on in the work of the Lord,
    that you may trample upon all deceit within and without.
    All you who are gathered together with the light
    and your minds turned towards Christ Jesus
    who enlightens you, that you may all see
    the Lord Jesus among us, your Head,
    and you His branches:
    In the light waiting and growing up in Christ Jesus
    from whence it comes, you will bring
    forth fruit to the glory of His name.

All waiting and walking in the light,
    with it you will see the Lord Jesus among you.
    You will see with the light all that hate it,
    who profess Christ Jesus' words declared
    from His light, and walk not in it.
    By His light are they,
    and all their profession,
    condemned.

   And to you this is the word of the Lord.[44]

-Epistle 55, VII.70-71

---

[44] This phrase, like the phrase "thus says the Lord God," was often uttered by prophets to emphasize they were not speaking their own words, but a message given them straight from the Almighty. George Fox is, in effect, saying the same.

TAKE HEED OF RUNNING ON IN A FORM

Take heed of running on in a form,[45]
lest you do lose the power,
but keep in God's power and Seed,
in which you will live in the substance.

And in any disputes take heed.
Many may be lifted up in the victory
and conquest, and after have a joy
in the prophecies and openings,[46]
and after *fall.*

If babblers come, and janglers say
they have a bad meeting,
and so the murmuring nature gets up,
out of patience and the Seed
which bears all things and suffers
all things: which keeps down that
which causes lifting up, murmuring,
and disputing (which the Seed ends,
and prophecy, and keeps down all
the other that is contrary),[47]
and would live in the contrary:

---

[45] A form = a ceremony or outward ritual that lacks the inward presence and power of God.

[46] The prophecies and openings = the former are messages from God delivered by His prophets and the latter were revelations granted by God.

[47] The Seed = is Christ Jesus who ends prideful lifting up and disputing by His presence. He ends prophecy, because there is no longer need for men and women to bring a message from the Lord – Christ Jesus is present and powerful and can speak through whomever He selects. He, in His power, will keep down that which is contrary to Him.

That which keeps down that which
does change is the peace, cornerstone,
and the stayedness in the Seed and Life.

-Epistle 73, VII:166

CONCERNING THOSE THAT GO OUT
OF UNITY AND DENY FORMS[48]

Those that are gone from God's Light, spirit, and power,
yes, they being gone into their own wills
and into a perverse spirit,

then they say, they will not be subject to men's will,
nor to the will of man, and that spirit leads them out
of the bonds of humanity.

Then they say they will be not subject to forms,
and cry down all forms, with their darkness
and a perverse spirit, and so mash all together.

When they are thus gone from God's Light, power, and spirit,
they go out of all true forms,
into confusion and emptiness without form.

So from the unity, and by the Light, spirit and power
are they judged and the power, Light, and spirit are over them,
for there is a form of godliness, and a form of sound words.

---

[48] Forms = Form as used in this QuakerPsalm is different from form as used in the prior Psalm. In the prior instance, Fox was warning against falling into an empty action or ritual, one that is devoid of inward Truth, what too often happens in religion. In the present Psalm, he is speaking in much broader terms. Here he warns against denying the particular character, nature, structure, or constitution of a thing; the particular mode in which a thing exists or manifests itself, its due shape, proper figure, orderly arrangement, or good order. These forms are God given and to deny them is to sow confusion and leave people empty and confused. In our own time, the move to reject the essential form and nature of marriage leaves that relationship confused, empty of meaning, void. The same is true of our essential, God-given understanding of our human nature and condition. To deny our tendency to sin and do evil – to claim that we are fundamentally good – is to sow all manner of confusion on the personal level and on the social, policy, and governmental levels. Fox's insights are particularly profound and needed in our own age.

Many have a form.
All creatures have a form.
The earth has a form,

and all things were brought into a form by God's power
for the earth was once without form,
and was void, empty, and confused.

So they that be gone out of God's covenant and life,
out of God's power, are gone into a confused condition
without form, a state out of the bond of civil men and women.

Such are confused without the right form,
for the form that God made – of the earth,
of the creatures, the form of men and women,

the form of sound words and godliness,
the form of sound doctrine –
were never denied by God's men and women.

But such as got the form only,
and denied the power of godliness,
those were denied,

for they deny the power
and not only do so,
but quench the Spirit

and grieve and vex it
and hate the Light
by which Light they are condemned.

-Epistle 271, II:16-17

ALL MEMBERS...FROM THE HEAD
TO THE FOOT

All members who are joined together
by the Spirit of God and Christ their head
from whom they receive nourishment,
in the grace of God, are serviceable in the body.
God's Spirit does distribute to everyone severally,
as He wills, and so all are made to drink
into one Spirit, in which they have all fellowship

in the heavenly drinking of the spiritual drink
and eating of the spiritual bread
that comes down from heaven.
So every man and woman's eye must be lifted up
to heaven – and minds, and thirsts, and desires,
and hearts, and the soul that hungers,

the needy that sighs, and the poor that groans –[49]
for this bread comes down from heaven
and the spiritual drink that they may have,
the spiritual bread in their own houses,
and heavenly water in their own cisterns,
with which they have to refresh themselves and others.

-Epistle 313, VIII:69

---

[49] Not only the eyes, but all that is listed – all of us – must be lifted up to heaven.

LEST ISAAC'S WELL BE STOPPED BY THE UNCIRCUMCISED PHILISTINE

Let your faith stand in the power of God,
    for that is your keeper unto the day of salvation.
    Everyone that has not yet obtained it,
    come to that salvation's day,
    for the kingdom stands in power,
    and not in words.

Let your faith stand in the power of God,
    in which the kingdom stands,
    the kingdom of peace and joy,
    which stands in righteousness,
    holiness, and the Holy Ghost.
    No unclean thing enters, nor can it.

The power of God keeps you fresh,
    keeps you open, keeps you alive,
    keeps you in a sense of the things of His kingdom:
    the treasures, the pearls, and riches, and jewels thereof.

This power will keep you all in peace, in unity, and quietness,
    condescension,[50] love, and kindness one to another.

In the Lord's power and in His Spirit,
    you will be enabled to give the Lord His glory,
    and continual praise and continual thanks.

---

[50] condescension = as used here, does not mean "to look down upon with a superior attitude," or "deal with people in a patronizing, superior attitude." In 17th century England, it was often used to mean "graciousness, considerateness, or submissive deference shown to another" (OED).

And so none quench the Spirit nor the motions of it in you,
  lest Isaac's well be stopped by up the uncircumcised Philistine[51]
  who lived aloft, who must go down into the pit.

-Epistle 300, 8:48

---

[51] Isaac's well = Fox is referring to the wells in Genesis 26:17-26, the wells of Isaac's father Abraham, which Isaac is reopening, with some difficulty. Several wells are disputed by the Philistines, who claim "the water is ours" and Isaac in turn names them Contention and Enmity. However, at Beersheba, the Lord appears to him, saying, "I am the God of your father Abraham; do not be afraid, for I am with you and will bless you and make your offspring numerous for servant Abraham's sake. Here Isaac's servants dig yet another well and soon report "we have found water!" The story is emblematic of the on-going confrontation between those who live in the presence and power of God's Spirit and those who profess to, but are not faithful.

IN HIS WISDOM AND LIFE KEEP

I do warn and charge you
in the presence of the living God,
in His wisdom and life keep,
that no ill savor be
nor get up among you –
for you are the salt of the earth
to season and make savory to God,
but if the salt has lost its savor,
it is henceforth good for nothing.

Therefore I do warn you all,
mind that which does keep your peace,
whereby you all may grow in love,
and know Christ in you all,
in whom is peace.

You are the light of the world
to answer the light in every one,
that with the light they may see
your good works and seeing them,
they may glorify your Father
who is in heaven.

Everyone keep in the measure
of the life of God, for all deceit
is judged and condemned by it,
and see that there be no strife
nor presumption among you,
but all serve one another in love,
and let that of God guide every one of you,
in which you may have unity one
with another and with God.

In His life wait to receive power
to bind and chain all down
which is contrary to truth,
and so in God's life and power,
the Lord God Almighty
preserve you to His glory.
Amen.

IN HIS WISDOM AND LIFE KEEP
Postscript

The light is precious to him that believes
in it and walks according to its leading,
for the light and the Truth were before
darkness and deceit were.

So, while you have the light,
walk in the light and live in the light –
Christ the Truth – that you may,
through obedience to it,

be the children of the light and of the day.

-Epistle 156, 7:148-149

Never Give Over Seeking the Lost

In which we consider,
➢ *The work of ministry and those called to ministry,*
➢ *The different kinds of ministry,*
➢ *How we are all called to seek those who were lost or driven away*
➢ *And how we must never give over seeking the lost,*
➢ *How we are to keep atop of the mountains of sin and oppression*
➢ *And bring forth spiritual pearls,*
➢ *How we are to bind and fetter wild natures so the Lamb may get the victory,*
➢ *With a warning to those who have known Truth and turned away,*
➢ *And how the Truth will stand over them that hate it,*
➢ *How Christ will remain and God's seed will be over all.*

THE MINISTER'S WORK

The minister's work is to go from house
to house and warn all both small and great,
yea, with tears.

This is the word of the ministry in the Spirit –
in the Spirit that gave forth the scriptures
and so brought people into the life

that gave them forth, with which
they were able to instruct one another,
and to stir up the pure in one another.

The work of the apostles, the ministers
of the gospel, and Christ, was to bring people
into the life that gave forth the scriptures,

and into the substance, Christ Jesus, that
the scriptures testified of. But you who are fain
to seek the life and substance in the letter,

in the letter of scripture for it
and have it not from within,
are never like to beget to God.

TO THE LABORERS IN GOD'S LIFE, TRUTH, AND POWER

1

The laborers in God's life, Truth, and power
labor in God's vineyard and have their heavenly penny,
that everlasting treasure. So see that
you have it. If you be in the labor
of life, you will have it.

Friends, see how men and women can speak
enough for the world, for merchandise,
for husbandry, the ploughman for his plough,
but when they should come to speak for God,
they quench the spirit and do not obey God's will.

But come! Let us see what the wise merchants
can say: Have they found the pearl and field,
and purchased the field that yields those glorious
glittering pearls? Let us see what you can say
for God and that heavenly merchandise:
What can the ploughman with his spiritual
plough say for God? Is the fallow ground ploughed up?
Has he abundance of the heavenly seed
of life? What can the heavenly husband say:
Has he abundance of spiritual fruit in store?
What can the thresher say? Has he gotten
the wheat out of the sheaf, the heavenly
wheat, with his heavenly flail? Let us see,
what can the spiritual ploughman, husbandman,
thresher say for God? How they have labored

in the vineyard, that they may have their penny.

2

Some are breakers of clods in the vineyard.
Some are weeders. Some cut off the brambles
and bushes, and fit the ground, cutting up
the roots with the heavenly axe for the seed.
Some harrow in, some gather and lay up

the riches. Here are the merchants, ploughmen,
harrowers, weeders, reapers, threshers in God's
vineyard. Yet none are to find fault one
with another, but everyone is to labor
in their places, praising the Lord, looking

to Him for their wages, their heavenly
penny of life from the Lord of life. None
are to quench the spirit, nor despise prophecy,
lest you limit the Holy One. Everyone
is to minister as he has received grace,

which has appeared to all and brings salvation,
so that the Lord's grace and light and Truth
and spirit and power may have the passage
and the rule in all men and women, that
from it in all He may have the glory.

-Epistle 275, VIII:20-21

SEEK THAT WHICH WAS LOST
AND DRIVEN AWAY

All you believers in the heavenly Light
as Christ has taught, seek that which is lost
and driven away.
The false prophets, ministers, and teachers
did *not* seek that which was lost and driven
away from God.[52]
They put no difference between the precious
and the vile, but mash all together
like the priests and prophets of our time.
Seek that which was lost and driven away.
Some may be driven away by the storms,
some by the great winds of the wicked, some
by the tempests and foul weather. Some may
be lost in the foul weather and the sea of the world.

Seek that which is lost, you that believe in
the Light by which you see and are distinguished
from the false prophets and teachers.
Jacob[53] was found in a desert and see
the prophets, how they sought that which was lost,
and the apostles, and how Christ encouraged
to seek that which was lost. When the lost sheep
was found, what joy there was, more than
of the ninety and nine.

---

[52] A central and most damning characteristic of false prophets, ministers, and teachers is that they do not seek those who are lost or driven away. They may pursue political ideologies and agendas, dubious gospels, or even their own self-aggrandizement. True ministers and teachers know that there is no substitute to replace Christ Jesus' Great Commission.

[53] Isaac's second son to whom Esau sold his birthright as first son: Jacob received by trickery the aging and blind Isaac's blessing, but later wrestled with God's messenger in the desert. He becomes the man through whom the promises of God to Abraham descend, instead of the unfaithful first born Esau.

Who are they that make the land desolate,
but the rough Esaus, wild Ishmaels, and Cores?[54]
And who makes the world as a wilderness,
but the devil? And who brings the whole world
to lie in wickedness, but the devil, the wicked one.

If you should not find that which is lost
at the first, nor second, nor third time of seeking –
if you should not find him that is lost –
go again that you may have your joy
and rejoice others. When any such come back,
they will tell you how hungry they were,
how they could never fill their bellies
with the husks while they went astray.
They will tell you long declarations
of the citizen they were joined to.

When the lost is found and brought back again
to the Father's house where there is bread
enough, there is joy, and the heavenly
musical instruments, the heavenly feast
of heavenly fat things, and the heavenly robes
of righteousness. So all be diligent,
as Christ has taught you, you believers in
the Light. Look up and down: in the Light
you will see where the lost sheep are
and such as have been driven away.
You will spy them out, out of the woods,
or brambles, or pits, where there is no water,
where they are ready to be famished,
where they are tied with thorns and briars.

---

[54]Esaus, wild Ishmaels, and Cores = Inward states exemplified by Esau, Ishmael, and Core in the scriptures. Esaus are those who sell their spiritual birthright and toss away their life with God for the cheapest of pleasures. Ishmaels are those who act like wild asses. Cores are those who speak against the Truth, God's will, for the purposes of gain.

So with the Light you will see
and put a difference between the precious
and vile, and you will see how the false prophets
and ministers and teachers drive people away:
They drive them away from God, and His way,
from Christ, and the covenant of Light.
How angry they are with them that believe in it!
With their clubs, they have beaten many, wounded
many, imprisoned many, because they
would not be driven into the devil's pit-fold!
But do you never give over seeking,
for the Light shines over all who believe
and walk in the path of the just, which is
as a shining light. This has been the way
of all true ministers, to bring them to feed
in the pastures of life and gently to lead them,
whose ways are life, and He gives them their
heavenly penny of life eternal.[55]

-*Epistle* 266, 8:11-13

---

[55] A reference to The Parable of the Workers in the Vineyard, each of whom is paid a
denarius or penny for his work (See Matthew 20:1-16),

NEVER GIVE OVER SEEKING THE LOST

If you should not find that which was lost and driven away,
    at the first, nor the second, nor the third time of seeking:
If you should not find him that is lost, go again,
    that you may have your joy and rejoice others,
for Christ in the parable says: "the prodigal son was lost,
    yea, was dead, and is alive again,"
        when he had been feeding among swine,
            and upon husks, and could never fill his belly.

When any such come back again,
    they will tell you how hungry they were –
        they could never fill their bellies among the husks –
            while they went astray,
    and will tell you long declarations of the citizens
        they were joined to.

When the lost is found,
    and brought back to the Father's house,
        where there is bread enough, there is joy,
        and the heavenly instruments of music,
        the heavenly feast of the heavenly fat things,
        and the heavenly robes of righteousness.

So all be diligent, you believers in the Light, as Christ has taught you.

Look up and down. In the Light you will see where the lost sheep are,
    and such as have been driven away.
        You will spy them out, out of the woods,
    or brambles, or pits, where there is no water,
        where they are ready to be famished,
            where they are tied with thorns and briars.

T.H.S. Wallace

Do you never give over seeking,
    for the Light shines over all which believe in
        and walk in the path of the just,

as you may see Christ and the apostles and all the true prophets did
    to bring them to feed in the pastures of life,
        and gently lead them.

-Epistle 266, II:12-13

KEEP YOUR FEET UPON THE TOP
OF THE MOUNTAINS

To messengers of His covenant of Light

All moved of the Lord by His power, Light, and Life,
to go into other nations to preach the gospel,
as messengers of His covenant of Light,
according to that which shows the secrets
of every man's heart, wherein nations
are brought into the covenant with God,
and redeemed out of tongues, people, and kindred:

keep your feet upon the top of the mountains,
and sound[56] deep to the witness of God in every man.
Then will your feet be beautiful, that publish peace.
To the captives proclaim liberty, with your feet
upon the mountains publishing peace,
binding up the broken-hearted,
having oil of gladness for them that mourn.

And this is the word of the Lord God to you:
keep you atop of the heads of all mountains
of sin and opposition, in innocence,
meekness, and true humility, in the fear of God,
that in His dread and wisdom, you may
be kept, and in the fear of the Lord stayed.

---

[56] Sound = This word carried not only the meaning of declaring or speaking, but also the meaning of probing (like a crew member sounding or measuring for the river or ocean bed, The term may also suggest the qualities of being solid, healthy, fit, morally correct, as in "of sound body and sound mind."

DO YOU DIG FOR YOUR PEARLS?
BRING THEM FORTH!

Do you labor in the vineyard? Do you
minister and speak forth the things of God?
Do you dig for your pearls? Bring them forth!
Let them be seen how they glister,[57]
the glistering pearls.

All[58] come into the vineyard of God to labor,
in the Light which was before darkness
and with the Life which was before death
and his[59] power was. All come into God's vineyard
in His Truth and power, which the devil is out of,
that everyone of you may have your penny,[60]
that precious penny and heavenly treasure.

Mark: The laborers in the Life, Truth, and power
of God have their heavenly penny, so see that you have it.
If you be in the labor of Life, you will have it.
What can you say for God and the heavenly merchandise?
What can the ploughman say for God with his
spiritual plough? Is the fallow ground ploughed up?
Has he abundance of the heavenly seed of Life?
What can the heavenly husbandman say?
Has he abundance of spiritual fruit in store?
What can the thresher say? Has he gotten
the wheat out of the sheaf, the heavenly wheat
with his heavenly flail? What can the spiritual
ploughman, husbandman, and thresher say for God?

---

[57]glister = shine with a bright light, brilliance, luster.
[58] This is a key point – everyone has a role in ministry and in the work of the Kingdom
of God. Note some of the many listed and suggested by the Vineyard metaphor.
[59] His = death's.
[60] See note 55 – another reference to The Parable of the Workers in the Vineyard in
Matthew 20:1-16.

Some are breakers of clods in the vineyard,
some weeders, some cut off the brambles
and bushes, fit the ground, cut up the roots
with the heavenly axe for the seed, some
harrow in, some gather and lay up the riches.
So you may see: here are merchants, ploughman,

harrowers, weeders, reapers, threshers in God's vineyard,
yet none are to find fault with one another,
but everyone labor in their places, praising the Lord,
looking to Him for their wages, their heavenly penny of life.

-Epistle 275, VIII:20-21

GET THE YOKE UPON THE WILD HEIFER, KEEP THE BIT IN THE WILD HORSE'S MOUTH

To Messengers of His Covenant of Light

The Lord God Almighty keep you in His power and wisdom
    and by it bind the unruly.
When you have bound them, then you may speak to them
    and by it fetter them.
Then you may catch them when you will,
    when they are fettered.

Get the yoke upon the wild heifer.
    Then you will save yourselves from a push,
    and bring them down,
    order them with the power,
    and reach to the witness.[61]

See that you keep the bit in the wild horse's mouth,
    whereby his head may be held down.
    See that he be bridled;
    Then with the power he will be ordered.
    Though he snuffs and snores[62],
    the bridle being kept in his mouth,
    he is held down by it
    (though he cries "aha, aha!" – he
    that would be above the witness).

---

[61] The witness = is what early Quakers called "that of God in everyone." It was not a divine spark to which they referred (the spark idea was a 19th century recycled neo-platonic idea from ancient times), but the thirst or longing or need for God which found its fulfillment in coming into the presence and will of Jesus Christ. Quaker preaching pursued the goal of "reaching" the witness.

[62] Snores = not a misprint for "snorts," but means the same thing. It also means a harsh and noisy respiration from the month. Both meanings fit quite well.

When this is done, being kept in the power,
    you will know Him that rides meekly
    upon a colt to Jerusalem,
    the highest place of worship:
    He who brings the prisoner out of the pit,
    where there is no water –
    Christ, the same today as yesterday and forever.

The Lamb gets the victory. He that sits meekly upon the colt:
    He it is that gets the victory,
        He by whom the world was made,
            who is not of the world,
                that treads upon the highest worships in the world.[63]

-Epistle 195, VII:185-186

---

[63] The highest worships in the world = refers to man-made forms of worship, awe inspiring liturgies and rituals, which have no foundation in Christ Jesus. That is, they are not "worship in Spirit and Truth," but man created activities that are not necessarily focused on worshipful waiting to come into the presence of Christ, come to know His will, and come to follow Him in obedience. The key to the phrase is "in the world," meaning the worship is worldly, not heavenly, in nature.

TO THOSE THAT HAVE KNOWN THE
TRUTH AND TURNED BACK

All you that have known the way of Truth, tasted of the power of the same,

> and now turn back into the world's fashions and customs:
> You stop them that are coming out of the world;
> you make them to stumble at the Truth;
> you make them to question the way of the Lord,
>> which is out of the way of the world and its ways.
> You grieve the righteous and sadden the hearts of the upright and simple.

You had better never have known the way of Light, life, and power:

> You are the cause of many keeping in darkness.
> You are the cause of the boasting of the wicked
>> and make the wicked to take you for an example,
>> their object[ion] against the Truth and them that live in it,
>> to plead against its ways.

You had better never been born.
> *Your days will be sad; trouble and vengeance*
> *will be your garment and clothing in that state.*

> A hard thing it will be for any of you to repent
>> for you will bind a more subtle thing in you than was
>> before you knew the way of Truth,[64]

---

[64] While today's readers may mistake George Fox's statements here for vengeful threatening, they are not. He is simply emphasizing a spiritual truth: those who have known the way of Truth and turned back not only cause great damage to others, both faithful and worldly, but also they "will bind a more subtle thing" in themselves than before they knew Truth. Jesus speaks of this same spiritual truth in Luke 11:24-26: "When an evil spirit comes out of a man, it goes through arid places seeking rest and does not find it. Then it says, 'I will return to the house I left.' When it arrives, it finds

you who have neglected hearing the voice of God,
    through which your hearts are hardened.

You will cause many husbands and wives, and servants and children
    thereof to boast themselves against the Truth,
    for in some families, there are servants convinced,
        children convinced,

    and in others there are husband convinced and not wife,
        wife and not husband, servants and not masters,
        children and not parents.

You that turn from the Truth,
    you are the object[ion] for them that are not convinced
    to turn against them that are.

Woe and misery is for you!
    You had better never have been born
    nor known the way of Truth,
    whose latter end is worse than the beginning,
    when the way of peace is hid from your eyes
    and a place of repentance you cannot find,
    though you wash your altar with tears;
    whose latter end is worse than the beginning,
    being in the stained life where all the tattlers,
    tale-carriers, unclean persons, murmurers
    and complainers are, [being] out of the life,
    power, and wisdom of God, which has
    the royal dominion and possession of the Royal Seed.

---

the house swept clean and put in order. Then it goes and takes seven other spirits more
wicked than itself, and they go in and live there. *And the final condition of that man is worse
than the first"* [Italics mine].

Therefore, turn! Turn all that are not hardened and past feeling:[65]
  Hear the Voice, that the way of peace and repentance,
    the way of life and salvation, you may know and live in.

Upon all your disorderly carriages, walkings, words, and actions,
    you may come to receive judgment
    and through that you may receive power to live in new life,
    in which God is served in the Truth,
    and not the devil who is out of the Truth.

In the Truth are the holy unity and the pure dominion,
    the everlasting life promised and received,
    and the Royal Seed, which the elect have,
    wherein they have the Bread of Life.

-Epistle 211, VII:210-211

---

[65] It is clear by this statement that this Psalm is not condemnation without the hope of repentance and mercy. Though repentance in this state is much more difficult, it is not impossible, for all things are possible with God.

THE TRUTH WILL STAND OVER
THEM THAT HATE IT

The Truth is above all and will stand
over all them that hate it,
who labor in vain against it,
and will bring their own house
on their own heads to their great trouble.

In the winter and cold weather,
when their house is down, their religion frozen,
their rivers dried up, their husks gone,
and the swine begin to cry about the plantations –
and vermin run up and down among their
old rubbish, their sparks and candles are
gone out, and hail and storms light upon the head
of the wicked, then woe will be to Gog
and Magog,[66] and to all the wicked
who have no covering.

In Christ you have peace,
in the world you have trouble.
No peace with God can be enjoyed
but in the Covenant of Light.
Without it: trouble.

-Epistle 294, 8:44

---

[66] Gog and Magog = the nations, led by Satan, that will war against God's kingdom. Rev.20:8: "When the thousand years are ended, Satan will be released from his prison and will come out to deceive the nations at the four corners of the earth, Gog and Magog, in order to gather them for battle." This gathering ends in the doom of Satan.

THE SEED THAT
WILL REMAIN

You that know the light of Jesus Christ
and have tasted of His power,
by which you come to be gathered
into the name of Jesus:

Do not forsake the assembling
of yourselves together,
but provoke[67] one another,
and exhort one another to love
and to good works.

Let not powers nor principalities,
nor prisons, thrones, nor dominions,
spoiling of your goods, mockings,
scoffings, nor reproachings,
and pluckers off your hair,
and smiters, separate you
from the love of God
that you have in Christ Jesus
who conquered death and the devil,
the power of it, the adversary,
the wicked one, the enmity.

---

[67] Provoke = While we think of provoking as meaning to goad someone into anger or a fight, it also has positive meanings, meanings that Fox is using here: to summon or invite, to call forth or urge (OED).

Being gathered into Christ
and into His name, keep your meetings
in the power of God and in His light and life,
whose gathering is above all other gatherings.
Feel the seed of God which was before
that which makes to suffer[68], the seed
that will remain when it is gone.

-Epistle 205, Works, *VII:201*

[68] That which makes to suffer = evil and persecution.

FEEL GOD'S SEED OVER ALL

Feel the Seed of God over all that which is in the Fall,
    that is gotten up since Adam
    and Eve fell from righteousness
    and God's image – and in which Fall
    the Lamb has been slain.

Feel the Seed of God over all that which makes to suffer,
    the Seed that will stand and remain
    when he that makes to suffer is gone.

So feel Christ to reign and rule over all that which is in the Fall,
    and there you may all feel the life
    to flow over all, which life was
    with the Father before the world began,
    and will remain when death and its power
    are gone. In that life live and dwell,
    and in it keep your meetings.

And feel the word of patience and the word of wisdom,
    in which you may find both patience
    and wisdom in this day of life.

And feel my love to all Friends in God's everlasting Seed.

-Epistle 174, VII:166

I am Compassed about with Pure Virgins

I AM COMPASSED ABOUT WITH PURE VIRGINS

In the power and in purity's bed,
in the singleness of virginity,
and in the beauty of holiness live,

where righteousness, holiness, and Truth
dwell together, and peace in the kingdom
of power. Live where the everlasting joy,

peace, dominion, and victory are,
where the bed is not defiled, but the marriage
that is honorable is known. In that live.

I am compassed about with pure virgins
and the undefiled ones are my joy.
The virgins trimmed with oil in their lamps,

enter in with the bridegroom. All you virgins
pure, lose not the ornaments of the Lord,
but wait, that you may be married to the Lamb

in the everlasting marriage and remain
with Him in the world that is without end.

-Epistle 74, VII:85

APPENDICES

*1. THE
IMPORTANCE
OF TYPOLOGY
2. BRIEF
DOCTRINALS
3. A NOTE ON
THE LIFE AND
FAITH OF
GEORGE FOX*

APPENDIX 1

THE IMPORTANCE OF TYPOLOGY IN QUAKER FAITH AND IN THE QUAKER UNDERSTANDING OF THE SCRIPTURES

A.T. Hanson, in his article on "Typology" in *The Oxford Companion to the Bible,* defines it as "the practice in the New Testament and the early church whereby a person or a series of events occurring in the Old Testament is interpreted as a type of foreshadowing of some person (almost invariably Christ) or feature of the Christian dispensation."[69] For instance, Abraham's willingness to sacrifice his son, Isaac, is a type or figure of God's own willingness to sacrifice His son. Another example is God's redeeming Israel from slavery in Egypt, a figure of His redemption of spiritual Israel from sin and death, through Jesus' sacrificial death and resurrection. Such parallels abound and led both early Christians and early Quakers to conclude that typological interpretation was a useful help in reading the scriptures and grasping the deeper significance of events in the Old Testament. The very use of typology by the writers of the New Testament gave early Christians and the first Quakers solid justification to pursue it in their own efforts to understand Scripture.

Typological interpretation depends on the Christian and Quaker understanding that the Scriptures portray the nature and course of salvation history, an understanding based on the legitimate assumption that God works always with His redemptive purpose in mind. Quakers readily accepted this fact, given their experience and faith that God and Christ are the same yesterday, today, and forever – and that they are not changeable. And Quaker acceptance of typology was reinforced by the understanding that the writers of the various books in Scripture were inspired by God's Spirit. Thus, the inspired words of Old Testament writers logically bear a deeper meaning than those writers may have been aware of – a deeper sense that is revealed in the New Testament. The

---

[69] See George Fox's own use of typology in his declaration on *Salvation History,* p.13-16.

first generations of Friends added one proviso concerning the reading of the Scriptures: that they must be read in the same Spirit that inspired their writing. It is God Himself that reveals the inner meaning and application of the Scriptures. The words in the Bible are merely the letter and need the addition of the Spirit to bring them and their readers fully to Life.

Further study: See uses of typology in the Old Testament in Isaiah 43:1-19 and 51:9-11. Examples of New Testament typological use appear in Peter 3:19-21, Hebrews 11:17-19, 1 Corinthians 10:1-11

APPENDIX 2

A CLUTCH OF SHORT DOCTRINAL PSALMS

These short works are drawn from Fox's *Doctrinals*, of which he wrote 4 volumes. I include a small selection of doctrinal psalms here, because of the startling clarity with which they define the early Quaker understanding of some central Christian concepts.

JUSTIFICATION AND CONDEMNATION

A man that is justified by God
is not condemned by his own conscience,
for the mystery of faith is held
in a pure conscience
and a man that is condemned
in his own conscience, is not justified
in the sight of God. That which condemns
is the light, and the cause of condemnation
is the hating of the light, not believing in it,
the cause that conscience comes to be seared.

WORDS AND THE WORD

The scriptures are the words of God,
the words of Christ, and so not The Word,
but the words which The Word Christ fulfills.

They that hear The Word of God,
hear that which lives and endures forever,
which they have within them;

And with that they see the words,
and letters, writings, outward tables
may be broken, but still The Word remains.

Those who are in the faith are made
wise to salvation through the scriptures,
and come to Christ the end of them,

for faith gives to see the scriptures
and in faith is the unity.

-3:145

T.H.S. Wallace

WHAT HUMBLES PEOPLE
AND BRINGS DOWN THE SIN

Sin is that which does not humble,
but lifts up. What humbles people,
and brings down the sin, is the humility
which bears the sin and iniquity: Christ.

The saints were made free from sin
while they were upon the earth,
and had the body of sin put off.
They who have received the divine

nature, know it, and have escaped
the pollutions and lust that are
in the world, and so the divine
nature destroys sin in its being.

Vol.- 3:412

ON SEEING AND NOT SEEING GOD

Your lives and conversations must preach righteousness
and holiness, for without holiness none shall see God.

And going into unholiness, that is
the cause that none see God;

And the cause why there is not peace
among a nation or people is,

they do not live and walk in righteousness,
but walk and follow the unrighteous spirit,

which is out of Truth. Christ says, "Blessed
are the pure in heart, for they shall see God."

Therefore, keep in God's pure spirit, that does
mortify all impurity and unholiness,

which blind people from the sight of the pure God.

PERFECTION IN THE CREATURE IS CHRIST

The doctrine of perfection in the creature is Christ,
    who destroys the devil and his works, and binds
    the strong man and spoils his goods,
    and takes the possession of it to Himself –
    and the creature is a perfect creature,
    out of transgression.

"He that is born of God does not commit sin,"
    seeing God's seed remains in him – and that
    is the doctrine of perfection in the creature.
    Christ makes all things new and you that deny Christ
    cannot witness anything made new, are in the old things,
    crying up imperfection.

- Epistle 357, VIII:194-195

APPENDIX 3

A NOTE ON THE LIFE AND FAITH
OF GEORGE FOX

Today's historians often term George Fox the founder of the Religious Society of Friends, better known to the world as the Quakers. However, he, himself, would have said that he was commissioned by His Lord to call people into the pure faith of Christ Jesus, the prophets, and the apostles – the faith of the early Christians. His *Journal* and the two volumes of his *Epistles* are classics of Christian writing.

Coming of age in the North of England in a time of great religious and social upheaval, Fox began an intense spiritual search that led him to consult many of the great preachers of his day and to become so thoroughly familiar with the Old and New Testaments that he knew nearly the whole of them by heart. What he discovered during this search was a Christianity splintered into warring factions, most grasping for State power, while the nation's individual parishes served largely to guarantee a "living" for the sons of aristocrats, - a living based on a State/Church tax called the "tithe." The majority of ministers and priests so supported had little interest in, or understanding and experience of, the faith they were supposedly preaching and they often crassly distorted or baldly misinterpreted Scripture for their own dubious and deceitful ends.

George Fox's spiritual search led to a series of openings or revelations from God, revelations that emphasized how corrupt, misguided, and shallow the Christianity of his time had become. The first opening he received concerned "how it was said that all Christians are believers," both Catholic and Protestant, but if all were believers, then they were all born of God, and had passed from death to life, and...none were true believers but such; and though others said they were believers, they were not" [*The Journal of George Fox*, Nickalls edition, 7]. Fox saw that being educated "at Oxford and Cambridge did not qualify a man to be a minister of Christ" and that Fox, himself, if he was to walk rightly, would have to rely wholly upon the Lord Jesus Christ [*The Journal,* 8]. "At another time," Fox tells us in his *Journal,* "it was opened to me that God, who made the world, did not dwell in temples made with hands…, but that his people were his temple, and he dwelt in them" [8]. The more Fox studied his Bible, the more he saw that there "was an anointing within man to teach him, and that the Lord would teach his people himself," the very definition of the New Covenant presented in Jeremiah 31:31f. By 1647, Fox had left the priests and preachers of his day, "all those called the most experienced people," for he "saw there was none among them all that could speak to my condition" [*Journal,* 11]. It was then, he tells us:

> When all my hopes in them and in all men were gone, so that I had nothing outwardly to help me, nor could tell what to do, then, Oh then, I heard a voice which said, 'There is one, even Christ Jesus, that can speak to thy condition,' and when I heard it my heart did leap for joy. Then the Lord did let me see why there was none upon the earth that could speak to my condition, namely, that I might give him all the glory; for all are concluded under sin, and shut up in unbelief as I had been, that Jesus Christ might have the preeminence, who enlightens and gives grace, and faith, and power.

These early revelations culminated in 1648 with Fox's commission to "proclaim the day of the Lord." "Now," he tells us:

> I was sent to turn people from darkness to the light that they might receive Christ Jesus for to as many as should receive him in his light, I saw that he would give power to become sons of God, which I had obtained by receiving Christ. And I was to direct people to the Spirit that gave forth the Scriptures, by which they might be led into all Truth, and so up to Christ and God, as they had been who gave them forth.

In this passage, Fox emphasizes the reason why so many of the "Bible-believing" Christians of his day failed to understand the Scriptures rightly, pursuing State power and violently persecuting one another. They had the Scriptures, but without having the same divine Spirit by which they were written, people could not correctly understand the Book.

So began one of the great ministries in the history of Christianity, one in which Fox declared the good news, that Christ has come to teach and lead His people Himself. Fox traveled throughout England and Wales, on the European continent, in Ireland, and from Georgia to Massachusetts, these latter travels only fifty years after the founding of the Jamestown Colony in Virginia. George Fox, though a man of great physical strength, suffered greatly over the forty years of his ministry. As he traveled and declared the gospel in the early years of Puritan military rule of England (1640s to 1660), his life was repeatedly threatened and he was often severely beaten. With the re-establishment of monarchial government in England in 1660, treatment of Fox and the Quakers hardly improved. Thousands were imprisoned. Others were repeatedly fined for attending meetings for worship and ministering in them, the use of fines being designed to destroy Quakers economically. Imprisoned eight times for preaching and meeting for worship outside the State Church, he (and his fellow Quaker ministers – men and women alike) worked repeatedly for freedom of conscience to worship God, an effort that led to the founding of Pennsylvania in 1681 by Quaker William Penn, with its guarantee of religious and political freedoms (after which the U.S. Bill of Rights would be modeled in the 18th century).

George Fox died in 1691, finally worn out by the rigors of his ministry, its long imprisonments, beatings, and extraordinary travels. Active until the last, we are told that in worship "he declared a long time very preciously and very audibly and went to prayer." However, after worship, he complained of cold, went to bed, and soon after expired. "According to the witnesses" at his passing, "his going was contented and appropriate to his life. They heard him declare, 'I am clear, I am fully clear.'" The great work of the Lord in his life was finished and he passed in peace.

For further study of George Fox and the faith he declared, readers have *The Journal of George Fox,* the John L. Nickalls edition being the finest short version.[70] It is best approached with Joseph Pickvance's *A Reader's Companion to George Fox's Journal* published by the Quaker Home Service in London, 1999. Pickvance's introduction is an excellent help for the reader unfamiliar with the history of 17th century England, 17th century English, and the relevance of George Fox's ministry to our world today. Those who desire to pursue the subject in greater depth will find that a CD-ROM of the eight volume *Works of George Fox* will be available at the end of 2010, by the publisher of this volume. *QuakerPsalms* and *None Were So Clear: Prophetic Quaker Faith and the Ministry of Lewis Benson* (the latter on the life and scholarship of one of the foremost Fox scholars in the 20th century) will also help the reader who desires to come more deeply into early Quaker faith, experience, and practice.

-*T.H.S. Wallace*

---

[70] I do not recommend Rufus Jones' edition of *The Journal*, because of its many misinterpretations of Fox's ministry, preaching, theology, and mission.

CPSIA information can be obtained
at www.ICGtesting.com
Printed in the USA
BVHW032333210322
632031BV00003B/77

9 780970 137548